COUNT THE ANIMALS!

WELCOME TO

COUNT THE ANIMALS!

GOOD LUCK!

COUNT THE BEARS!

There are 5 bears!

1   2   3   4   5

CAN YOU COUNT THE **CATS?**

1 2 3 4 5

There are  cats!

6 7 8 9

ARE THERE MORE BEES OR LADYBIRDS?

With **9** ladybirds

and **10** bees

There are more <u>bees</u>!

1 2 3 4 5 6 7 8 9 10

HOW MANY **FROGS** CAN YOU COUNT?

There are 4 frogs!

1   2   3   4

COUNT THE SEA CREATURES!

1   2   3   4   5   6

There are **12** sea creatures!

7   8   9   10   11   12

COUNT THE ANIMALS WITH SCARVES!

There are 8 animals with scarves!

COUNT THE PIGS!

1   2   3   4   5

There are 10 Pigs!

6   7   8   9   10

ARE THERE MORE **BUTTERFLIES** OR **SNAILS?**

With  9 butterflies

and 7 snails...

There are more <u>butterflies</u>!

1 2 3 4 5 6 7 8 9

CAN YOU COUNT THE <u>DOGS</u>?

1

2

3

There are 6 dogs!

4

5

6

COUNT THE PENGUINS!

There are
Penguins!

1 2 3 4 5

CAN YOU COUNT THE **FISH**?

1 2 3

There are 7 fish!

4 5 6 7

COUNT THE ANIMALS WITH BEAKS!

There are 5 animals with **beaks!**

1   2   3   4   5

ARE THERE MORE CRABS OR STARFISH?

There are 8 crabs and 8 starfish...

So there's the same amount for both!

1 2 3 4 5 6 7 8

COUNT THE
CREEPY
CRAWLIES!

There are  creepy crawlies!

1   2   3   4

CAN YOU COUNT THE BIRDS?

1   2   3   4

There are 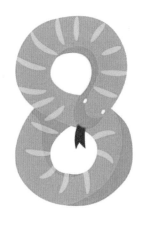 birds!

5   6   7   8

CAN YOU COUNT THE **SHEEP**?

1   2   3

There are **6** sheep!

4   5   6

COUNT THE ANIMALS WITH <u>WINGS</u>!

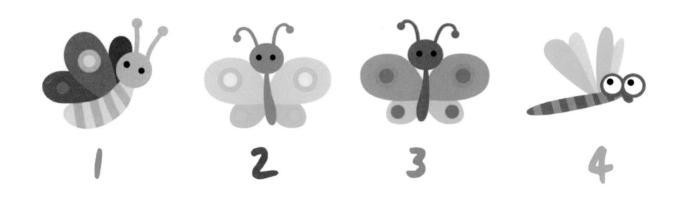

1   2   3   4

There are **8**
animals with wings!

5   6   7   8

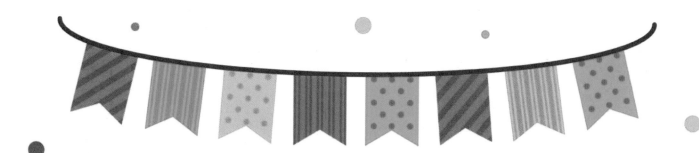

THE END!

BOOKS for little ONES

Find us on Amazon!

Discover all of the titles available in our store; including these below...

Made in the
USA
Middletown, DE